1001 STUPID REASONS
TO NÆME YOUR KID

Version 1.0

Greg Dent and Jeff Welker

For our kids, Balthazar and Nefertiti

Epidemic Books Co.

Seattle, WA - USA

http://www.epidemicbooks.com

This embarassing mockery of literature, we regret to say, is published by Epidemic Books Co. Ltd.

Epidemic Books Co., The Epidemic Logo, and 1001 Stupid Reasons are trademarks of Epidemic Books Co. Ltd. ©2016 Epidemic Books Co. Ltd.

Goat art by Todd Morasch

Don't get the joke? Riddle hints are available from Epidemic Books via our website.

First Edition, August 2016 - Made in the United States of America

You know how it goes, you've spent literally months carefully agonizing over your very special kid's very special name that you are sure is going to make her the very most special person in the entire world, and then she comes home crying after her first day of school and tells you the other kids spent all day making horse sounds at her. Where did you go wrong?

OK, let's clear a few things up. It's not actually your fault; there's nothing wrong with your kid's name; you could have named her Jennifer and everyone would still hate her. It's just that your very special kid is actually just an awkward, sniveling little whiner, and nobody likes her. See, kids are cruel little geniuses, and can take literally any name and make fun of it if they want to ostracize someone. Heck, the kids making fun of your kid are all named Hermione and Madison themselves—pot, meet kettle.

So anyway, if you are going to walk into a firefight, it's best to be prepared, so read on reader, and sally forth and arm yourself with an avalanche of useless knowledge. With this book fully under your belt, you will be entirely forewarned as to what sorts of nasty encounters your kid may find himself drawn into because of the terrible choice you made before he was even born.

And for you first timers out there, you are probably here because you've spent literally months agonizing over your very special kid's very special name, and come up with zilch. Your brain is Fred, and you need something entirely idiotic to jump start it and get it running again. You want a name that actually means something to you, but at this point you have given up on it meaning all that much. You have come to the right place as well.

So here's how this works: you have a nameless kid, and we have a book of names. Each name has a yes/no question associated with it—a riddle of sorts. Read the question, and if you answer yes, well then the name attached to the riddle is yours for the taking. Occasionally the riddle doesn't fit the pattern, but if you like the joke, that name may be for you.

We actually find it's best to have someone read the questions to you aloud so you can't cheat and look ahead and see the answers. This works best sitting on a back porch in August on a swing chair with a Pomeranian in your lap and a mint julep in your hand (or maybe an ice tea if you're still knocked up). Of course, having your friend scream the questions at you as you blaze down the highway at 70 miles an hour in your fully-restored, chocolate-brown Ford pinto while listening to death metal works too. Jesus, as long as you buy the damn book, people, we don't give a crap.

Just don't pick Hortense.

BOYS

Do eggs make you angry?
Greg

Do you have a favourite toe?
Tobias

Does your house look like a bear lives there?
Larry

Did your barber cut your hair too short today?
Bob

Tired of sitting on your ass?
Stan

Have you ever wanted to take a trip
to see the great wall of china?
Walter

Feeling sick?
Earl

Is there an unusual number of prostitutes
in your town compared to most?
Horatio

Need a little spice in your life?
Herb

Do you like to eat your apples down to the nib?
Corey

Are you honest to a fault?
Frank

Did you finish that gingerbread girl?
Oliver

Do you buy way too many lotto tickets?
Maximilian

JFK conspiracist?
Noel

Wake up in the morning ready to conquer?
Norman

Do you like to wear vintage clothes?
Donald

Cut yourself shaving?
Nick

Do you cut gems for a living?

Joel

Do you ever wonder if your baby
will turn out to be a reprobate?
Woody

Are you frequently weaving your friend's hair for
them?

Braden

Do you like the old times?
Julian

Does your work offer a great health care plan?

Benny

Have you ever dug someone a shallow grave?
Barry

Love New England in the fall?

Leif

Is your phone always ringing?
Collin

Do you love it when people bow down before you?

Neil

Do you always get stuck carrying the casket at funerals?
Paul

Are you a nudist?
Jay

Does it feel like you're always getting fleeced?
Jason

Did your dad snort coke?
Pablo

Do you often wonder what that smell is?
Theodore

Obsessed with orgasms?
Theo

Worried your unusual combination of genes
will make your kid too odd?
Todd

Did you finish 50th at the grand prix in Rome?
Carl

Are you rather hirsute?
Harry

Are you never satisfied?

Moe

Deep in debt?
Bill

Is July through November your favourite time of year?

Jason

Love butter?
Pat

Are you a sauerkraut on rye kinda person?

Reuben

Live in a high crime neighborhood?
Robin

Are you a perpetual embarrassment to your family?

Seamus

Did you serve in the army?
Barack

Does Christmas always feel repetitive to you?

Samuel

Always making mistakes?
Aaron

                              Would you say you've got a bit
                              of a drill sergeant personality?
                                                        Titus

Do you have to walk through the mud a lot?
Claude

                    Love to watch old black and white horror films?
                                                        Gregory

Right handed?
Dexter

                    Always borrowing woodworking tools
                    from that wise guy next door?
                                                        Alexander

Do you think a criminal record is a
badge of honor of sorts?
Conrad

                    Always respectful of elder homosexuals?
                                                        Sergei

Spend too much money on your hair?
Frodo

Think hydroelectric power is the best?
Adam

Used to be an artist but got arthritis?
Drew

Are you going to plant sweet potatoes this year?
William

Do you have to diagnose psych patients?
Hussein

Used to work on a ranch?
Brandon

Feeling claustrophobic?
Preston

Did you key that speedwagon?
Mario

Yoga buff?
Matt

Are you disgusted by men?

Ishmael

Do you have a habit of swindling
money out of your mom?
Connor

Are you hungry?

Hoagie

Do you work out a lot?
Jim

Do you like camping but hate roughing it?

Harvey

Do you like to lay down grout?
Tyler

Do you copy that?

Roger

Finally found your life's work?
Colin

Always butting heads with people?

Warren

Overdoing it on the pickles?
Dylan

                              Love pulling pranks on your dad?
                                                  Patrick

Do you tend to drone on and disinterest others?
Boris

                         Do you have an overly long commute?
                                                    Homer

Tend to overeat?
Phil

                                        Drive a gas guzzler?
                                                   Phillip

Ever fantasize about Burt Reynolds naked?
Robert

 Do you agree that France is a wonderful place to visit?
                                                  Francis

Do you admit that you were kind of a jerk?
Benedict

Need some help with that bag of groceries?

Zachary

Do you always keep your phone unlocked in case
you stumble upon the perfect photo op?
Cameron

Use the bathroom a lot?

Lou

Would you say you are capable of anything?
Abel

Are you a know it all?

Ken

Do you walk with a limp?
Cain

Think you've got a better body
than that dude over there?

Abdul

Have a song in your heart and
don't care who knows it?
Humphrey

Are you proud of how many
baby seals you clubbed last year?
Michael

Trying to get the thunder God's attention?
Jesus

Are you a minimalist?
Les

Feel like your vote doesn't count?
Chad

Do you enjoy hard Canadian butter candy?
Mustafa

Find yourself frequently placating authority?
Sherman

Buy a lot of disposable goods?
Chuck

Think life would be simpler if
you just skipped Christmas?
Ulysses

Do you have an unusually high sex drive?
Randy

Drawing a line in the sand?
Vito

Do you make the best soup?
Stewart

Does your physical lifestyle tend
to be rough on your clothing?
Terrence

Do you bow down before gold?
Troy

Do people think less of you because of your lisp?
Luther

Spend your free time huffing lemon pledge?
Dustin

Do you make your own fruit preserves?
James

Does an e-flat grate on your nerves?
Tony

Do you love karaoke?
Mike

Have a habit of being brusque?

Curt

Are you terrified of spelunking?

Kevin

Sick of that boil?

Lance

Do you ever worry about people
slipping anything into your drink?

Mickey

Would you like to hike along a pleasant wooded
valley beside a calmly trickling brook?

Glenn

Does the thought of haggis excite you?

Scott

Are you a car buff?

Otto

Are you easily persuaded by other people?

Gavin

Do you frequently yell at your spouse
from the couch to get you a beer?
Johan

Do you like hamlet?
Toby

Do you think you could handle it if I hit you?
Howard

Have you ever set your pants on fire?
Bernard

Like coffee with your donuts?
Duncan

Are you a clumsy jerk?
Rudolf

Feel like a big wheel?
Axel

Like eating turkey?
Tom

Often find yourself deleting something you just typed
then typing it again and then deleting it again?
Reynold

Do you tend to tell falsehoods
in your electronic mail messages?
Eli

                                    Feeling generous?
                                            Grant

Do you enjoy painting or drawing women?
Arthur

                        Do you enjoy a good striptease?
                                            Jesse

Are you a connoisseur of diamonds and rubies?
Jules

            Have you ever tried to disguise or distract from
            some damage to an item you were advertising?
                                            Marcel

Do you prefer urinating outside?
Pierre

                        Do jail showers appeal to you?
                                        Lawrence

Feel like one-upping that six over there?
Sven

Love kicking back with a few cold
ones after you've been in a fight?
Bruce

Partial to the shoulder bag?
Percy

Like military haircuts?
Jared

Like the look of natural brick?
Mason

Are you an ass man?
Heinz

Are you a complete and utter tool who hates his kids?
Jermajesty

Have you spent the weekend
rocking out with your buddies?
Benjamin

Do you kid around a lot with your friends?
Josh

Are you ready, willing and able?

Igor

Are you a French mathematician?
Leonard

Nauseous?

Ralph

Do you scream "Come at me, bro!"
at the germs of the world?
Daryl

Do you have prematurely white or grey hair?

Harold

Do you just love pie?
Barry

Often find yourself trying to reassure older
gentlemen that it's OK for them to use
their money to buy the things they want?

Spencer

Enjoy s'mores?
Graham

Trying to quit smoking?

Lester

Ever have that dream where you are
being chased by some horrible monster?
Ron

Like opening doors for regal ladies?

Damon

Believe in the 3 second rule?
Jeremy

Do you show respect to your social betters?

Millard

Do you always feel a little hint of pride
after finishing washing the dishes?
Jordan

Love sports replays?

Schlomo

Do you have a speech impediment
and work out too much?
Thor

Do you like lasers?

Ray

Can you change a tire like a pro?

Jack

Down a quart?

Rusty

Don't think the earth is round?

Vlad

Never seen a pair of pants that big?

Eugene

Are a crossdresser?

Tucker

Finally finished your turtle sculpture?

Sheldon

Would you lick a cactus for 100 dollars?

Alex

Is your vocabulary too big? Find yourself
always having to explain when you
use fancy phrases like "in lieu of"?

Louis

Do you enjoy going down to the
dump and shooting at cans?
Martin

Do you think fresh leafy vegetables are overpriced?
Richard

Feel like you're wasting away?
Wayne

Hate it when the doctor puts that stick in your throat?
Noah

Always bumping into things?
Luke

Cheating on your spouse?
Tristan

Feel like you have everything you
want in life, just not enough of it?
Moses

Love pesto?
Basil

Got a statue of Zoe Saldana out front?
Alonzo

Is your uncle a transvestite Latino?

Antoine

Are you a graffiti artist?

Mark

Do you aim for the ankles?

Logan

Ever tried to catch your flatulence?

Ferdinand

Do you love the sunshine days of spring?

Meriwether

Did that orgasm not go the way you hoped?

Malcolm

When people say things like "special ed"
or "physical ed", do you actually think
the "ed" part is a real word?

Edward

Have you ever attempted to train a fish?

Edgar

Proud to be married to your wife?

Herman

Love surfing the biggest waves?
Maxwell

Do you play scrabble with someone
who hogs all the vowels?

Yuri

Are you the local limbo king?
Solomon

Does your computer never work right?

Fritz

Doest thou ever thinkest thou hast no allies in life?
Timothy

Do you think streets should be called A B and C
instead of having randomly ordered names?

Blaine

Looking for a place to hang your steak?
Dmitri

Do you tend to make sloppy passes
at single ladies when you are drunk?
Hamish

Were you born between July 23rd to August 22nd?
Emilio

Do you collect old spares?
Tyrone

Do you punch your enemies in the junk?
Paolo

Do you find widows sexy?
Garret

Do your cats go nuts for improvisational music?
Jasper

Like to go whale watching during birthing season?
Calvin

Spend a lot of time in the bathroom?
John

Are you always surprised when your
friends cry at maudlin movies?
Giuseppe

Are you a skilled archer?
Beau

Are you sick of waiting for them to get
around to making "legally blonde 3"?
Maurice

Think cremation is the way to go?
Ash

Dig McDonald's new healthier menu options?
Mikhail

Do you have a perverse hairpiece?
Ludwig

Just starting a long drive?
Milo

Practice a lot with your crew team?
Rowan

Do you like just chilling in the garden?
Noam

Like assembling Ikea furniture?
Allen

Suddenly sprouting massive amounts of hair?

Grover

I f you somehow acquired a fortune
in animal fat, would you try to maintain
it to pass along to your descendants?
Willard

Do you always finish the last bit of chicken noodle?

Supinder

Have you read every last Tolkien book there is?
Alfred

Do you have a habit of talking about
father Christmas when you are drunk?

Stanislaus

Do you take everything to the extreme?
Max

Like tossing leafy greens at unsuspecting people?

Caleb

Does your portrait make you look really good?
Dorian

When you look in the mirror can you just
not resist giving yourself a hearty greeting?

Jaime

Do you get easily frightened by
night sounds while camping?
Russell

Are you really bad at first person shooter games?

Ezekiel

Do you tend to agree with people more when stoned?
Truman

Can't wait to finish that huge painting?

Merle

Do you drive around in an oversized
car that you insist is not a minivan?
Donovan

Are you surrounded by mean spirited jerks?

Charles

Can you speak Quenya?
Elvis

Would you like it if Jesus finally
accepted your invitation to tea?
Christopher

Do you tend to scream at the tv when
you are watching football in your man cave?
Daniel

Ever can't decide whether to punch someone in the
nuts or knee them in the nuts and end up doing both?
Hannibal

If you were stuck in a lifeboat with a robot,
would you let the robot do all the work?
Arturo

Have you ever replied to an email about a chicken?
Henry

Approve of the work librarians do?
Sean

Think Australia should secure its borders?
Oswald

Do you have a secure place in your home where you
lock away your rock and mineral collection?
Joseph

Think you can train your kid like you train a dog?
Sid

Are you short and Jewish?
Lloyd

Did Santa think you were one of the bad kids?
Cole

Are you just missing a hammer?
Armand

Did you try pulling a fast one on your teacher
by swapping places with your identical twin
but got a crummy grade anyway?
Cody

Do pea pods make you horny?
Gregor

Always laughing out loud?
Lowell

Love being a paper pusher?
Clark

                                    Think you've overscratched that rash?
                                                                    Ezra

Ever go skydiving with a German?
Andre

                            Really good at remembering sequences of colors?
                                                                    Simon

Is your cargo hold not quite full yet?
Morton

                                                    Are you a marathoner?
                                                                    Miles

Need some kind of spiritual leader to direct your life?
Amos

                                            Prefer to lease rather than buy?
                                                                    Randall

Like wearing fancy athletic supporters?
Jacques

Do you judge people based on their handbags?

Percival

Were you really into the little girl next door growing up?

Douglas

Good at turning attacks back at your opponent?

Perry

Really good at following people?

Taylor

Have a really strong bolt on your front door?

Sherlock

Trying to perfect your foghorn leghorn impression?

Isaiah

Big fan of inland seas?

Errol

Did you lose five cents?

Nicholas

Ever incorporated lunchmeat into your magic act?

Abraham

Think that dude in the center square is all washed up?
Lyndon

Did you decide not to go out for dinner last night?
Aidain

Did you barely make it before the doors closed?
Justin

Love eating albatross innards?
Gulliver

Would you rather:
A) Get a paper cut on your eyeball,
B) Eat a live scorpion
C) Jump into a pool of used needles
or
D) Pull your own fingernails out?
Ethan

Do you hate birthdays and lie about your age?
Arnold

Do you work in research and development?
Artie

In the habit of asking others to pass you the joint?

Jamie

Fan of the chiefs and royals?
Casey

Are you a bit rough on your possessions?

Rex

What are you doing, Dave?
Hal

Fall in love easily?

Cliff

Do you demand to be treated like royalty?
Leroy

Do you snore like a lion?

Rory

Are you a sycophant?
Yasser

Are you tough and stringy?

Chuy

Ever thought life might be better in a pouch?
Joey

Are you constantly talking about your possessions?
Ivan

Giving the thumbs up to the local
district attorney's reelection?
Diego

Almost, but no cigar?
Klaus

Dig beer?
Stein

Did you just volunteer to take over the ship?
Wilhelm

Gave your husband permission to play D&D?
Maynard

Are you Kenny G's less talented cousin?
Luigi

Fascinated with the diaspora?
Jerome

Ever crossed swords with a sandwich?

Hiro

Are you always dredging up old arguments?
Harper

Ever opened a door with your mouth?

Keith

Have you ever really thought about archery?
Beauregard

Prefer to get your information on a monthly or
weekly basis instead of daily or on tv?

Magnus

Does your wife make you drive her everywhere?
Carter

Have a nice set of pearly whites?

Dennis

Are you a fatalist?
Mort

Are you a sport fisherman? Or a Hemingway fan?

Marlon

Are you the leader of a bunch of
ragtag Norwegian P.O.W.'s?
Haakon

                Having second thoughts about buying a Chevy?
                                     Rutherford

Have you really let yourself go?
Ichabod

                             Do you move a lot?
                                Roman

Are you a British quarterback?
Ike

                Like touring the country in your mobile home?
                                     Irving

Can you still remember the serial
number of your first girlfriend's car?
Earvin

                         Did you get busted out of jail?
                                     Gottfried

Have you got one of those 26.2 stickers on your car?
Myron

Saving for your retirement?
Ira

Did you hate Pygmalion so much
you threw rocks at the stage?
D'Brickashaw

Are you really angry about having to do the
same damn thing over and over and over?
Rutger

Were you totally unsuccessful at laying down
new shingles on your house?
Raphael

Ready for the hoe-down?
Fidel

Are you metric through and through?
Graham

Do you have sticktoitiveness?
Kip

Do you think the former vice president
has worn out his welcome?
Gordon

Do you like buying stuff on sale?
Clarence

Are you going to have a taxidermist
take a gander at your gander?
Gustaf

Do you avoid eating cabbage and garlic?
Fergus

Another spot of earl grey for you, dearie?
Morty

Are you putty in other people's hands?
Plato

Wondering where to put your false idol?
Thaddeus

Are you sought after by the Hollywood set?
Oscar

Ever hear a falsehood so nasty it makes you
want to scream about it to everyone
(particularly your southern friends)?
Lyle

Do you like it when people ask you your opinion?
Paul

Do omeletes make you queasy?
Ignatius

Are you always trying to grab
that girl you have a crush on?
Caesar

Are you always on-message?
Jermaine

Are you a waiter?
Trey

Do you have a good grip on things?
Holden

Do you prefer looking up how-to instructions online?
Emmanuel

Love singing the star spangled banner?
Jose

                         Think irradiating milk is a good idea?
                                              Murray

Did you spill red wine on your beautiful dress?
Austin

                    Get annoyed when people ignore your emails?
                                                Maury

Are you a terrible singer?
Waylon

                         Do you believe in the power of prayer?
                                              Eamon

Do you have the small, beady little
peepers of a slippery bottom feeder?
Elijah

                              Do you prefer milk and eggs
                         from the American heartland?
                                              Darius

Can't decide between Stewart or Astley?
Roderick

Do you tend to buy off-brand or expired meat?
Grady

Didn't you ride that beast of burden to work yesterday?
Samuel

Do you look like an ape?
Simeon

Do you snore heavily?
Sawyer

Do you boycott genetically modified foods?
Gino

Do you find going to synagogue utterly dull?
Boyd

Ever looked at the number on your phone and declined to answer?
Khalid

Did you bore a peephole to spy
into the girl's locker room?
Seymour

                              Do you love cowboy movies?
                                                Weston

Seriously, you can digest wood chips?
Trevor

                              Do you hate deep water?
                                                Wade

So, did your tea date with the queen go horribly
wrong?
Travis

                              Are you a librarian?
                                                Reed

Are you a scotch fanatic?
Pete

                              Are you sunburned?
                                                Crispin

Think MTV was better when
they actually played music?
Vijay

Buying another civic to go with your accord?
Mohandas

Are you found on roads daily?
Ford

Taking a pottery class down at the community college?
Clay

Are you the funniest person in your cell block?
Brigham

Did you make extra sure you clamped
the paddles onto your kayak?
Orson

Ever wondered how come email addresses
have that funny symbol in them?
Wyatt

Can't get enough from Mr. Philips?
Maximo

Are you a massage therapist?
Hans

So, you're really not mad anymore?
Everett

Thinking about inventing pirate meditation?
Omar

Do you like palm trees
Franz

Are you a fan of Japanese horror films?
Ringo

Are you happy when Elmer Fudd is happy?
Dwight

Do you love Tic Tac Toe?
Marco

Are you stuck on someone?
Elmer

Do you want your Jamaican friend to spill the beans?
Montell

Can you hear the guns?

Fernando

Does it feel like you are always tired?
Jan

Prefer grass-fed beef?

Grayson

Did you survive a midair collision?
Eric

Do you think petroleum jelly

is the answer to everything?

Vassily

Do you wish you could open a
cafe to serve batman's foes?
Archimedes

Does the heat really take it out of you?

Wilt

Want your baby to be born in the
same town you were born in?
Salman

Remember that look on your face
when you passed that kidney blockage?
Winston

Do you blow exorbitant amounts
of money on anything you buy?
Peyton

Are people always parking next to you?
Kirby

Did you get here by paddle power?
Knut

Nonplussed by appetizers and desserts?
Andre

Are you always on the lookout for a big white one?
Moby

Would you describe yourself as
large, deep-voiced, and horny?
Angus

Your bomb didn't go off?
Dudley

How about this weather, huh?

Clement

Do you find sex very calming and reassuring?
Placido

Does cleaning carpets just really do it for you?

Vaclav

Hail from down under?
Ozzy

Does surrealist art make you drool?

Miroslav

Want to see the pyramids before you die?
Niles

Do you believe in the restorative
powers of Orville Redenbacher?

Cornelius

Need to turn around?
Huey

Do you flee formication?

Antonio

Touchdown?
Enzo

Are you Irish and love hitting things with sticks?
Harlan

Does the whole BDSM lifestyle just gross you out?
Dominic

Really really need to clean your feet?
Tomas

Think everything started tasting better once you
moved to that natural uncooked foods diet?
Rahm

Trying to outbid the other guys to become
Trump's new contractor and really rake it in?
Waldo

Oh shit, are you choking??
Heinrich

Are Lee Harvey Oswald and John
Wilkes Booth amongst your heroes?
Gunnar

Seriously, you're changing your locks again?
Keanu

Got oil on your land?
Derrick

So your personal trainer wants to know
what you are going to work on next?
Matthias

Do you run a pigeon farm?
Cooper

Feel like a Viking?
Norris

Are you a kick ass shortstop?
Mitt

Ever plugged a power strip into another power strip?
Channing

Tired of waiting around?
Owen

Do you run a textbook company?
Edsel

Ever have that dream where you are
standing on top of a bear, a beaver, a
wolf, and there's an eagle on your head?
Tatum

Are you twice the wrestling fan as the next guy?
Nelson

Got a runny nose?
Hank

Has everything just gone great for you lately?
Benito

Distracted while cooking over an open flame?
Sirhan

Always get randy when you think
about Ivan the terrible and all the
things you would let him do to you?
Balthazar

Got a shelf on your bookcase that has
"On Human Bondage", "The Moon and Sixpence",
"The Painted Veil", and "The Razor's Edge"?
Monroe

Got it easy in life?

Riley

Did the heater go out in your monorail?

Bertram

Enjoy showing off your estate to your heirs?

Aldus

Always a bit unprepared for
what life throws your way?

Ethelred

So how'd that fight go with that dude's hand puppet?

Wenceslas

Is your favorite musical "the wiz"?

Esau

Do you live in an open air pavilion?

Wallace

Sometimes, do you just feel like
767 mph isn't quite fast enough

Mahmoud

Have a dog grooming business?

Paco

Have you ever been busted for racketeering?
Rico

Is gluttony your favourite sin?

Emil

What are those chunks in your chop suey?
Amit

Are you a depressive dominatrix?

Saddam

Do you get a rash when you eat sushi?
Ichiro

Have a special shorthand you
use with your local French baker?

Kwame

Did your try out for that Quebecois
acrobat troupe go off without a hitch?
Xerxes

Is this conversation over?

Bubba

Is the lever on your toaster pushed too far to the right?

Saintjohn

Do you prefer being compensated in fish eggs?

Pedro

Like to drive fast?

Hollis

Want your kid to think about his father
every time he says his name?

Hassan

Do you suffer from rosacea?

Rasheed

Always surrounded by swarms of tiny little bugs?

Mitch

Dig those hard-boiled detective novels?

Dick

Ever played the grandmaster tournament circuit?

Chester

Do you frequently regret your outbursts?
Rufus

Really, you don't want a beer?

Bruno

Have you been through hell?
Dante

You're serious, aren't you?

Ernest

Every made a fundraising call from the bathroom stall?
Jonathan

Think they should base a theme-park
on the "Six-Million-Dollar Man"?

Leland

Regret not wearing that padded bra?
Rupert

Are you overly competitive?

Victor

Is your back so hairy you have to style it?
Virgil

Wondering if that damn laptop
is going to be delivered today?
Wendell

Are you the type that like to write everything
down, compare it, and check it off?
Alistair

Are you a proud uncle in a loving relationship?
Anthony

Are you a magnet for angry birds?
Brock

Always asking for the check?
Cassius

Do you host a mean late night show
and look good in a fur diaper?
Conan

Still sportin' that Ol' Dirty Bastard tattoo?
Declan

Do you live on a flood plain?
Duane

                    Ever tried to spray paint "Spuckbeutel"
                    on a Berlin train, but had it pull away
                    just as you were getting started?
                    Esteban

Has anyone ever paid you to give them cunnilingus?
Felix

                    Ever wonder why Dallas isn't still on TV?
                    Gerald

Seriously, we're actually there yet?
Finlay

                    Will you watch whatever garbage you can
                    find on the internet because you are too
                    cheap to sprint for a Netflix account?
                    Fredrick

Do you like to destroy things out of sheer boredom?
Hector

Do you... tend to... put... odd
dramatic... pauses... in your speech?
Kirk

Is your internet out?
Nolan

Own a mine or a record company?
Rocco

In a motorcycle gang?
Ryder

Do you react like a teenage boy
when you hear the word "boobs"
Stephen

Worked at that window company long
enough to cash in your stock options?
Sylvester

Proud of your degree from that women's college?
Wesley

Do you already have another kid named Adam?
Yves

Not the type to jump at every
bang, bump, and thump?
Colm

Have you always wanted to run a university?
Dean

Are you a knife-obsessed psychopath?
Dirk

Phone home a lot?
Elliot

Do you get your French and your Spanish confused,
but nobody calls you on it because you're the king?
Elroy

Sometimes do you just want to go somewhere nice
and hang out with all the spirits of the forest?
Fabian

Do you like to hide behind trees
so people can't see you?
Forrest

Are you the kind of person that spontaneously
invites random people to your events?
Jonas

Are you unusually pale and weak?
Juan

Do you try to sound extra casual when people
compliment your painstakingly selected outfits?
Otis

Into S&M and golf?
Cletus

Dig a man in a tutu?
Desmond

Think it doesn't make sense for programmers
to spend all their time in meetings?
Devon

Always follow the latest fashions?
Trent

Forgot your coat and just realized
it's starting to get cold?
Wilbur

Run out of gas all the time?
Gage

Totally don't believe your husband when
he told you who he was with last night?
Orion

Wait, that's it?
Saul

Tend not to run in a straight line much?
Ziggy

Like being in charge?
Abbas

So for some reason, Jerry Lewis is your butcher?
Floyd

Prithee sir, would you not say you are somewhat
obese?
Nathan

Having trouble keeping your head above water?
Adrian

Fuck "Intel Inside", amirite?
Cormac

Do you run into Akeem Olajuwon
all the time on your daily dog walk?
Joachim

Sick of this god damn low-fat diet?
Killian

Isn't that sweater rather itchy?
Raul

Oh oh, you've only got one piece left?
Reese

Think Darth Vader's where it's at?
Seth

Do you play hurt?
Soren

Does your stye leave people at a loss for words?
Uriah

Keep up with all the latest fashion crazes?
Zbigniew

Ooh, did you really get a chance to visit
that medeival siege weapon meusem?
Ramsay

Are you a pedantic nerd that feels the need to fill
the internet with criticisms of literally everything?
Enoch

A you a master with an epee?
Fenton

Still waiting for that Buck Rodgers/Smokey
and the Bandit mashup?
Gilbert

Do your parents own a patch of Scottish marshland?
Peter

Never missed an episode of that medicine woman
show?
Quincy

Do you still own all the Ernest movies on VHS tape?
Vern

Can never remember what burlap is made of?
Judah

Can't bear to watch when your team's down and just
keep asking your friends if they've caught up yet?
Steven

Like to go into the bushes and fake bloodcurdling
screams at 3am to freak out your nieghbors?
Nigel

Got a backdoor hookup for Mets tickets?
Shane

Nailed the landing off that balance beam?
Stig

Do you feel your pessimistic
attitude holds you back in life?
Kent

GIRLS

Are you uncomfortable around prostitutes?
Hortense

Love books?
Paige

Loved horses as a girl?
Mary

Think sea world should be shut down?
Lucille

Are you sure that's the same Ford econoline
that was parked outside the crime scene?
Vanessa

Sailing into the wind?
Lesley

Do you really like Barbie's other half?
Kendall

Not ready to buy?
Lisa

Not sold on the Toyota Camry?
Alexis

Reading the map upside down?
Pam

What's the best way to get out of here?
Doris

Do you frequently jump out of the tub yelling
"I found it" when a new idea hits you?
Erica

Can a certain taste bring you back
in time to your childhood?
Madeleine

Can you do skateboarding tricks?
Ali

Does the birthing process really excite you?
Natalie

Will you never go hungry again?
Tara

Sick of your Romanian accent getting
in the way of explaining your needs?
Ivana

Need a splint for that soccer injury?
Sinead

Feel possessive of the ~ symbol?
Matilda

Dig burgers?
Patty

Are you certain about that?
Shirley

Wondering if your mom is going to spend your
inheritance on coke and hookers or not?
Wilma

Have you faked your demise online?
Edith

Always singing a little higher than anyone else?
Octavia

Love lurking in the shadows?
Heidi

Think the imperial pint is the way to go?

Abigail

Dig those cool cats of the early 60s?
Maude

Like your eggs runny?

Yoko

So you have buck teeth and a flat ass?
Beverly

Looking for a way over that gap?

Bridget

Ever get your butt kicked so hard it left a shoe print?
Astrid

Always feel like the Aztecs get all the attention?

Maya

Do you ever feel a bit square?
Peg

Feel like you look like a cantaloupe?

Melanie

Think people who don't go for
the center square are idiots?
Linda

Were you ever a cheerleader?
Sarah

Like force feeding rude people?
Philomena

Like it when everything is fairly distributed?
Cher

Do you like fishing?
Annette

Do you have special undergarments
you wear on nights out?
Barbara

Were you a male cheerleader?
Laura

Do you subscribe to the whole
war on Christmas thing?
Mary

Think baseball was better back in the old days?
Ruth

Love the beach?
Sandy

Ever pirated a Courtney love album?
Nicole

Have a lot of aunts and uncles?
Denice

Not a "drink it out of the bottle"
kind of person?
Crystal

Are you not gonna go with the fender or the Les Paul?
Gretchen

If you forget that the cabinet is open
and hit your head, do you swear?
Dorcas

Text while you drive?
Vera

Like a nice sunrise and clean dishes?
Dawn

                    Does it drive you crazy when people
                    ask you if they can go to the bathroom?
                                                    May

Are you a bit on the litigious side?
Sue

                                        Like a fast car?
                                                Portia

Like a soft, creamy, crusted cheese?
Bree

                    Have to fly the whole cast and crew back to
                    Paris just to reshoot your film's ending?
                                                Francine

Can't think of a good sidekick
for your children's story?
Samantha

                    Start to make a horrible political mistake
                    but get slapped silly by batman
                    before you can finish your sentence?
                                                Electra

Living off your wife's paycheck?
Hermione

Are you always transferring your energy
via the direction of your motion?
Julie

Something in your eye?
Iris

Someone in the kitchen with you?
Dinah

Ever looked at cells under a microscope?
Cecilia

Do you ever secretly listen to Christmas music in June?
Carol

Do you already have sons named Cal and Gary?
Alberta

Believe in helping others in need?
Karen

Always getting stuck with the schlepping?
Carrie

Can't wait until springtime?

April

Do you bring fruit to your
grandmother for her to preserve?
Candace

Afraid of ending up a seamstress?

Sophia

Are you generally the object of everyone's attentions?
Desiree

Get groped a lot by clumsy fools?

Ophelia

Possessive of your conch collection?
Michelle

Do you always rush in before the pigs?

Pearl

So you sat through Pygmalion last night?
Sasha

Are the photos on your phone
always eating up all the space?
Dolores

Think Shakespeare was a fake?
Marlo

Like to hang onto the past?
Amber

Oh so you want a fucking lawyer huh?
Miranda

Do you have one leg shorter than the other?
Eileen

Are you always asking people for things?
Anita

Like mountains?
Sierra

Look a bit like Abe Lincoln?
Penny

Are you from Boston by way of Detroit?
Cassidy

Believe in Santa Claus?
Virginia

                           Do you love your cats so much you
                               tend to rub all the fur off them?
                                                           Petra

Don't want to just take some random book's
advice on what to name your child?
Prudence

                                            Do you want it all?
                                                          Olive

Do you live in a dump?
Lauren

            Got a bag of caramels hidden behind the couch?
                                                  Sacagawea

Feeling lost?
Maisie

                 Exhausted and ready for a good night's sleep?
                                                          Betty

Liked playing horsey with your pop as a kid?
Rhoda

Did you get perfect grades in school?

Anna

Are you overly demanding?
Juana

Like inviting your friends out to dinner?

Juanita

Do you scoff when people propose to you?
Maria

Just mopped but still need to wash the soap off?

Florence

Do you get almost feral and bitchy when you're angry?
Gertrude

Love syrup?

Mabel

Is your commute spent crammed into a sweaty
subway train with some lady's boobs pressed into
your back and some guy's ass in your face?
Titania

Seems like it was just memorial day
weekend a few months ago?

Megan

Hooked up to the power supply?

Ingrid

Ever made a profit on waterfowl?

Gisela

Don't want to watch the six million dollar man
marathon?

Leslie

Always keep your name-brand instant
coffee in an air tight container?

Sylvia

Do you always cut up your new pants
for that fashionable ripped look?

Jennifer

Can't bring yourself to step on that bug?

Jane

Do you own stock in the company you work for?

Sharon

Do badgers inspire you?

Harriet

Is your mama always freezing?

Heather

Think life's better once the sun goes down?

Eve

Need to vary your resistance but don't
really need to do it anytime soon?

Rhea

Ever stayed in a haunted hotel?

Evelyn

Prone to sharing your deepest thoughts like a Vulcan?

Imelda

She loves you not?

Daisy

Just watched the six million dollar man marathon?

Sally

Do you hate that bitch Anna?

Diana

Hated the six million dollar man
marathon so much you burned your tv.?
Ashley

Dump your trash straight into the ocean?
Marcy

What's that incessant ringing noise?
Isabelle

Do you like passing your germs around?
Cheryl

Did you find Pygmalion just a little too racy?
Natasha

Always cramming for that exam?
Tess

Got one of those circus mirrors at home to fool your
diet?
Selina

Like the old style New York city machine politics?
Tammy

Like a nice red berry in the winter, even if it's
poisonous and is covered in razor sharp leaves?
Holly

Still going through your sex change?
Juliet

Always wanted a chunk of France to call your own?
Britney

Hate it when your eggs stick to the pan?
Pam

Think that guy grinds corn in a very salacious manner?
Ludmilla

Is your mortal sin typically envy?
Chelsea

Do you eat the entire apple?
Coretta

Ever debated how much they probably
charged for a handjob in 1853?
Nicola

Spend a lot of time trying to get people
to go to your self-improvement seminar?
Celeste

Stocking up before Hillary takes them all away?
Morgan

Can you walk like an Egyptian?
Farah

Drive a fancy car?
Mercedes

Are you a British person fed up with trying to wash
your hands in American public restrooms?
Andrea

Do you spend much of your time
caring for your sick father?
Hilda

Sound like a horse when you laugh?
Winnie

So you and your friends bought some guns
and want to take down the government?
Melissa

Thinking about getting into the construction business?
Reba

Like to sing along to the stereo as you drive?
Carla

Are you of the "it'll all be ok in the end" type?
Faith

Are you a detective?
Katja

Do you think lovers spats are hilarious?
Tiffany

Ever get rageful with inanimate objects, such as doors,
when they don't function the way you want them to?
Dorothy

Got confused and genuflected in front of the judge?
Courtney

Think electric vehicles should be
able to use the carpool lane?
Elaine

Always up for a pancake feast?
Gretel

Always wanted to be wonder woman growing up?
Belinda

Sick of washing clothes all the time and hoping
your kid will take over that chore from you?
Yolanda

Are you a bit two-faced?
Janis

So your mouth is clamped open and your dentist
just pulled out the really big drill? Do you scream?
Olga

Trying to decide which daytime talk show to watch?
Eleanor

Having visions of your old dead granny?
Nancy

Do you lose yourself in the throes of passion?
Mona

Thinking about renting down in Florida?
Condoleezza

Ready for an open relationship?
Polly

Can't wait to get cremated?
Laverne

Not a fan of pulling into port?
Stacy

Can't stop thinking about that gondola
ride under the moonlight?
Venus

Love a good saxophone solo?
Jasmine

Have an urge to go for the nuts every time your
uncle Billy starts rattling off his favourite jokes?
Whitney

Like to play that rock and roll music really really loud?
Blair

Prefer the starchy stuff to the whole grains?
Beatrice

Do you go pale at the mere mention of childbirth?

Blanche

Spending a lot of time just lying on your bed staring up and wondering what to name your kid?

Celine

Secretly hoping to give birth on the elevated train?

Thelma

Pretty gullible?

Ruby

Was your mother a bit on the heavy side?

Fatima

Think Ziploc bags are the shizzle?

Priscilla

Are you always on everyone's mind?

Georgia

Chronic underbidder?

Lois

Sleep too much?

MacKenzie

Ever wager on the iguana races?
Lizbet

Still can't get enough Shaw?
Eliza

Accidentally scorched your brother's kid?
Bernice

Love knocking shit over?
Tipper

Not quite sure how you'd describe yourself
but there's way in 'ell you're normal?
Norma

Want to honor your pet that died of kidney failure?
Katrina

Fascinated by giant grapefruits?
Pamela

Just took a laxative?
Louise

Like a nice steady breeze?
Gail

Representing with your cheesesteaks?
Felicity

Ever heard a knock on your door, open it to find
a cosmetics salesman, and then slam it again
before she can even finish announcing herself?
Eva

Itching to try out that new magic spell?
Wanda

Are you small, round, have a thick skin,
but inside you're pretty sweet?
Clementine

Are you pretty conservative?
Tori

Don't tell me you lost that number?
Rikki

Do you look sweet upon the seat
of a bicycle built for two?
Daisy

Have you ever rapped a hip hop song about salad?
Leticia

Hate to say I told you so?

Cassandra

Like your south American pack animals long and lean?
Svetlana

Do you feel like a plaything?

Dolly

Does it bother you that people in general don't
eat meat with their hands anymore?
Fiona

Did that Italian lady tell you what
that hole in the wall is?

Isadora

Hey you, do you want schnitzel?
Mia

Is watching an old VCR tape of the
six-million-dollar man your way to relax?

Leah

Always wake up with morning wood?
Steffi

Would you describe yourself as humid,
gassy, and swarming with bugs and snakes?
Marsha

Are guys always screaming your name?
Stella

Got your handbasket?
Helena

Do you not bother to set out knifes
and spoons for dinner at your house?
Justine

Think all doughnuts should have filling?
Jillian

Do you like showing off all the
ridiculous wagers you make?
Betsy

Ever snorted corn syrup?
Caroline

Do you let your thoughts get away from you?
Imogen

Ever run away to get married in Pittsburgh?

Penelope

Does it feel like it just never fucking ends?

Constance

If given the chance, would you
eat corn chips at every meal?

Frida

Romanticize eating at greasy spoons?

Dinah

Don't believe in having kids out of wedlock?

Marion

Ever wished you could strap on a
feed bag and eat like a horse?

Hannah

Did you name your cat after
the six million dollar man?

Leona

Do you sometimes think of yourself as a 2x4?

Naomi

Never quite sure how to spell melee?

Emily

Think it would be fun to grow alfalfa
on the shore of a Scottish loch?
Agnes

Was your dad a lazy son of a bitch?

Alma

Didn't quite finish the law school entrance exam?
Elsa

Do you swear that guy from the center square
was in front of you in line at the supermarket?

Lindsay

Hate the thought of going back to
your job at the woodworking factory?
Mildred

Does your permissive attitude encourage
other people's bad behavior?

Anabelle

Wondering when you're going to start puberty?
Harriet

Love getting together with a group of friends and
going door to door singing Christmas favorites?
Carolyn

Dig exotic shellfish?
Conchita

Would your friends describe you as "a bit eccentric"?
Lupe

Looking for a butter substitute?
Marge

Feel like the weight of the world is on your shoulders?
Pilar

You're definitely pregnant?
Concepcion

Did you just enter the worst raffle ever?
Winifred

Ever had a pair of pants so ripped up they
looked like just a bunch of tattered strings?
Jeanette

Would you prefer to do most things at night?

Dana

Have a deep raspy voice from a lifetime of smoking?

Louisa

Ever visited the trinity college museum?

Kelsey

Like to go on long drives with your guy buddies?

Carmen

Thinking you might need to try Viagra?

Edie

Refuse to give in to the cable company?

Ariel

Do you tend to crack up in restaurants?

Lolita

Ever had your gelatin just not set right?

Nigella

Often find yourself asking someone
to pass you the cured salmon?

Lakshmi

Are you significantly older than your oldest sibling?
Esmerelda

Have you ever cried for me?
Suzannah

Not a fan of Pygmalion?
Shawna

Can't stop tweaking your manuscript?
Adeline

Is your lawyer a woman?
Shiela

Does it bug you when comedians lose their edge?
Stephanie

Never draw enough consonants in scrabble?
Val

Ever thought rap moguls would
make good advice columnists?
Dierdre

Like writing your name on the beach?
Sandra

Ever tried a pirate themed low-fat diet?

Arlene

Do you support those above you?

Joyce

Do you sing bass?

Lola

Are you a horror movie buff?

Tara

Can you explain the difference between
a cruller, an old fashioned, and a jelly?

Donatella

Have you ever owed anyone a smoke?

Bernadette

Does it disturb you how excited
horses get while eating?

Hazel

Do you have an extensive and well stocked cellar?

Wynona

Do you feel the rage of your ancestors burning
in your soul every time you even think
about bottomless breadsticks?

Cicely

Ever tried an all coffee diet?
Jolene

Are you a valley girl?

Lily

Love to knit?
Pearl

Did you used to be strong, at least?

Bronwen

In the market for a new laptop?
Adele

Need tech support for that new laptop?

Adelaide

Always wondered what Jesus was like as an
adolescent?
Christine

Ever tried to live with a British person?

Tegan

Managed to finish your dissertation and only
went through one pack of printer paper?
Miriam

Do you tend to heckle red heads when
you've had too much Tanqueray?
Ginger

Love driving south through big sur?
Carmella

Ever bought or sold an artificial joint over the Internet?
Melanie

Glad you weren't awake for your surgery?
Anastacia

Ever laugh at things when you are all alone?
Hillary

Are you a lefty?
Lucy

Do you feel like you are constantly
having to fix your roof?
Rita

Isn't it fun to talk like Peter Lorre?
Cherise

Would you be ok with being one of 700 wives?
Marisol

Wish you were you prowling the Serengeti?
Savannah

Straight A student?
Hester

Do you spend your free time thinking
up silly nicknames for your friends?
Monica

Living in drought country?
Maureen

Ever had your lover try that one thing that
felt really amazing right up until it didn't?
Monique

Think you are living in the most important
time period in the history of the world?
Kiera

Have you ever been assaulted by a swan?
Leda

Would you describe your baby's other parent as a god?

Demi

Think grandma's house is pretty dope?
Lacey

Think Jethro Tull would sound better underwater?

Gillian

Who wants pie?
Mimi

Are you more of a logical, inside the box kind of thinker?

Linnea

Would you call yourself a people person?
Gabby

Can't ever quite remember the lyrics?

Huma

Do you suffer from an overactive bladder?
Pia

Do you lose your shit anytime someone
mentions Pygmalion in your presence?
Aisha

Always wanted to do it on a boat?
Simone

Think diamonds really are a girl's best friend?
Gemma

Ever worked at radio shack selling cables?
Cordelia

Are you going to Scarborough fair?
Rosemary

Like to go whale watching and play the trumpet?
Darcy

Have a nasty habit of taking God's name in vain?
Lourdes

Think the concept of an eternal element
to human consciousness needs to be better
defined before you get behind it?
Solveig

Got a bit of a *sniff* habit?

Cokie

Do you relish in annoying your neighborhood
with your rousing rendition of amazing grace?
Piper

Think free will is an illusion, but that doesn't bother
you because life has something incredible in store for
you?

Destiny

Ever get drunk and tell EVERYBODY off?
Alia

Do you shrivel up in the sun?

Reza

Do you have a stye?
Soraya

Could you eat your weight in saag paneer?

India

Is Humboldt fog your favorite cheese?
Misty

Ever set a trap for a raptor?

Skylar

Do you just want those damn cheerleaders
to just shut up for one game?
Nora

Could you simply not imagine living
in a town that didn't have a wide array
of artisanal brined foods and beverages?

Brooklynn

Do you tend to babble?
Brooke

Do you find that you get less and
less done the older you get?

Sloan

Do you find it's more difficult to get
it up and keep it up as you get older?
Olympia

Are you a chocoholic?

Coco

Have that one neighbor who's always
parking his boat in front of your house?
Marina

Finally get that bolt unscrewed?
Lucinda

Ever thrown hot coffee in someone's face?
Jocasta

Think hockey's better off not trying to
clean up its body-checking habit?
Siobhan

Sunk your life savings into Japanese
currency and hoping for a payout?
Vivian

Ever bribed your professor?
Amy

So, you mean you aren't padding your brassiere?
Trudy

Ever needed stitches?
Sonja

Ever made a spliff?
Geraldine

                              Ever donated a dining set to goodwill?
                                                            Charity

Are you a breast cancer surgeon?
Nefertiti

                              Can't remember where you parked?
                                                            Carlotta

Oh my god, you just threw that lead pipe
at her head! Did you hit her?
Brenda

                              Does your artwork consist almost
                                    entirely of emaciated fairies?
                                                            Phaedra

Like to scream at the sunrise?
Danielle

                              Can't bring yourself to pay 4 dollars for a muffin?
                                                            Dale

Can't keep your fucking mouth shut?
Talia

Always disagreeing with your headmaster?
Nadine

Are you just a bit more inappropriate than the next guy?
Nadia

Are you nuts about anything gladiatorial?
Irina

Do you think Bulgaria is where it's at?
Sofia

Do you wish you'd marched with Dr. King?
Selma

Are your kids tired?
Tatiana

Hey, comrade, did the Soviet soccer team just score?
Golda

Think honey costs too much?
Phoebe

Would you be willing to pay half price for a
mail order mannequin with a defective leg?
Magdalena

Do you regret going to rehab for your ecstasy
problem?
Missy

Got a big booty?
Daphne

Got an itchy scalp?
Alice

Are you pretty agreeable to just about anything?
Kay

Are you always prattling on about
your crackbrain political theories?
Raven

Think smaller and faster is better
when it comes to antelopes?
Giselle

Skeptical by nature?
Aurelia

Are you a bit of an explorer?
Eudora

Hey who's buying dinner?
Sanjay

Writing down everyone who ever pissed you off
so one day you can finally get your revenge?
Callista

So you just got a new job thinking up fresh
new cereal ideas at General Mills and they've
already handed you an impossible mission?
Beatrix

Do you always head to where
the sale is in the supermarket?
Delilah

Are you a tiger in the sheets?
Malia

Would you be willing to attend a mosque
built next to Orange Julius and hot topic?
Malala

Do you find it very simple to greet a perfect stranger?
Heloise

Think Kipling would benefit
from more lumberjack scenes?
Kimberly

Do you think sex should feel like someone
is driving a chariot between your legs?
Hermione

Feel like you have little control
over where you are going in life?
Corrine

Have trouble sleeping at night?
Esther

Ever have someone cut you off in traffic
on the way home from your root canal?
Ethel

Are your forearms pretty much just
one giant mass of scar tissue?
Bathsheba

Are you more a nature over nurture person?
Deanna

Do you consider yourself oversexed?
Anya

> Are you a seamstress who isn't shy
> about charging for your service?
> Sophie

So you think you've finally discovered
the secret hidden messages in Pygmalion?
Keisha

> Don't you think there's just
> something off about that painting?
> Artemis

You're so vain, I bet you think
Beethoven's ninth was about you.
Joy

> Do you get paid to beat people up?
> Harmony

Think all good sins begin with gin?
Juniper

Ever seen Pygmalion on Christmas day in Guadalajara?
Felicia

Did you really burn a hole in your skin when
you spilled that Vietnamese soup?
Felicia

Wait, you really went to an Ivy League school?
Cornelia

Hey Bob Marley, what comes after D?
Iman

Have you got a secret desire you
are afraid to tell anyone about?
Cheyenne

Does drinking, dancing, and eating
haggis sound like your idea of a good time?
Kaylee

Do you work 9 to 5 at a tech company to
support your true passion: disco dancing?
Dakota

Starting a glossy monthly publication
about long haul trucking?
Maxine

Do you have an irrational fear that a monster will
grab you out of the tank in the portapotty?
Lucretia

Do you feel like you have to defend
that high ground at all costs?
Hildegard

Do you always hang out in front of the church?
Neve

Do you go to a twelve step program for
people who constantly forward emails?
Rhiannon

Do you own a convenience store
that caters to the underaged?
Martine

Are your fishing tools handmade by your grandma?
Nanette

Are you at your happiest when
you're telling "yo mama" jokes?
Gladys

Really digging that new conditioner?
Silke

Can't wait to get at that marrow?
Bonita

So, you finally kicked that smoking habit for good?
Sigrid

When people piss you off is your favorite method
of retaliation to spit right in their face?
Petunia

Do you feel compelled to chop your vegetables into
tiny little sticks when you cook?
Julianne

So, you have no idea what your
doctor is saying, but it sounds bad?
Amelia

Big fan of flash freezing?
Anais

Hate it when prissy people use the word brassiere
as if somehow makes their sentence less improper?
Sabra

Are you too loaded to spell loaded?
Elodie

                    Were you extremely sincere as an adolescent?
                                                      Ernestine

Huge fan of the Brady bunch Christmas movie?
Avery

                        Can you do that wiggle-your-nose
                        thingy and grant people's wishes?
                                                    Eugenie

Ever worked on a ranch in Canada in October?
Dorita

                            Did you go stag to your prom?
                                                      Bambi

Do you think there are ideas too deep
to be able to be conveyed with mere words?
Beyonce

        Ever worked at an aquarium training the morays?
                                                    Camille

Think there's no reason to buy the cow
if you can get the milk for free?
Chastity

Can you not say the words
"fava beans" without slurping?
Clarice

Are you planning to raise your baby as a Satanist?
Helga

Did you know Elvis is still alive?
Izzy

Would you thell your betht friend
out for forty piethes of thilver?
Judith

Were you on the cheerleading
squad in your Law School?
Lara

Are you livin' the Rasta lifestyle?
Marlee

What's the creepiest spectre you can think of?
Phyllis

God save the queen?
Victoria

Are you an optimist?
Hope

Do you seem to have a way of getting
on people's good graces quickly?
Indira

Are you kind of creepy?
Ivy

Do you practice good dental hygiene?
Flossie

"Angels We Have Heard on High" is hands down
the best Christmas carol, don't you agree?
Gloria

Do you have a crowded subway commute?
Joscelyn

Can't remember the lyrics, but you can hum it?
Melody

Really need to stop that horse?
Nelly

Are you a football fan from northern Cal?
Nina

That's not a real Coach bag, is it?
Persephone

Did you actually manage to get up this morning?
Rose

Is everyone always asking you for help?
Rhonda

You really don't actually give a damn, do you?
Scarlett

Can't remember which acid you dropped?
Tabitha

Do you just pretty much love everything?
Theodora

Think you can just add an "a" or something to the
end of the manliest name and make it instantly girly?
Wilhelmina

Are you a crybaby?
Willow

Do your friends say that you are overly relaxed?
Xochil

Too many daughters in your family already?
Addison

Pretty much think everyone in this galaxy stinks?
Andromeda

Never got the lead roles in your school
plays (or even the church ones)?
Angela

Committed to your diet, but the thought of that
triple-cream cheese in the fridge is just killing you?
Brienne

Refuse to call in sick to work,
even if you are actually sick?
Camilla

Does your brain pick the keyboard
bit out of any pop song?
Cynthia

Do you feel like anything you want to say has
already been said before by someone else?

Dido

Don't believe there's really a G-rated
David Lynch movie out there?
Gina

Pleasantly surprised when you flipped
through the channels and found the
"Six-Million-Dollar Man" marathon?

Hayley

So, you didn't rent a giant truck when you visited
Boston?
Jessica

So, you going to tell me your secret for how you
manage to stand in line for Star Wars for days
at a time without having to hit the bathroom?

Katherine

Are you a judge?
Layla

Can't get it out of your head?

Lynne

Is your sandpaper just not cutting it?
Margaret

Still pretending you're happy with your relationship
even though you are lying through your teeth?
Olivia

Proud of your noble lineage?
Patricia

Do you know what walks on four legs in the morning,
two during the day, and three legs in the evening?
Amanda

Think you need to burn the heck out of these low-fat
burgers to get them to taste like anything?
Charlene

Do you like to burn down your cigarettes really
carefully so you get that long, bendy char effect?
Aisling

Do you talk to your food?
Alicia

Admire how spiders capture their prey?
Antoinette

Got any home videos lying around
that you shot in Yosemite
Muriel

Is your dream to sing backup for
your favorite Caribbean pop star?
Adriana

Willing to pay a few hundred bucks a month
for life to always have a new car?
Alisa

Prefer a monkey puzzle to an oak?
Audrey

Do fatty foods like heavy cheese make you logy?
Briana

Can you hear me now?
Clara

Prefer to just let 'em hang when you get home from
work?
Deborah

Afraid to let that fart fly?
Erin

Is Egypt on your bucket list?
Kyra

                              Think history is bullshit?
                                             Lorelei

Is your birthday on Cinco de Mayo?
Maeve

                    Wish you could afford a sports car?
                                           Margot

Did nepotism get you that job at your dad's legal firm?
Paula

                    Like to cook your dad a big meal for
                 father's day to show your appreciation?
                                          Phillipa

Do you eat your hot dogs cold, right out of the
package?
Rowena

                    Planning to auction off your collection
                 of Six-Million-Dollar man memorabilia?
                                             Liesl

Thinking about throwing the most
badass Tupperware party?
Lydia

Find yourself constantly having to
explain why things happen to everyone?
Theresa

Are you a colonoscopy technician?
Camryn

Are you overbearingly sweet?
Chloe

Not afraid of the dark?
Elvira

Are you a Parisian vampire?
Genevieve

Does it feel like that constipation is lasting forever?
Guinevere

Think it was better in the old days when they'd
just chop off part of you if you got sick?
Ilsa

Simply don't want to forget that magical
night you spent in Galway?
Irene

Do you always have a cup of coffee in your hand?

Joan

Own a metal cookie box with a picture of Jesus on it?
Kristin

Got a bit of a limp after that
wallop you took yesterday?

Paulina

Always routing for David over Goliath?
Raquel

Think no means no, but sometimes you gotta
repeat yourself to get your message across?

Renee

Like your schnitzel undercooked?
Raya

Does tough meat make you cry?

Sabina

Prefer Polish to Finnish?
Valerie

Couldn't give a bucket of elephant's piss
what you end up naming your kid?

Zooey

Think it's time for a girl-centric Broadway
musical about Charlemagne?
Pippa

Are you all the rage among the vegans?
Quiana

Do you wait until the last minute to
put up your Christmas decorations?
Yvonne

Think you'd be able to handle a farmer's life?
Caitlin

Think everything sounds better when it's
harmonized by a hundred monks at once?
Chantal

Aw nuts, did that guy just scuff your giant sandwich?
Dagmar

Love listening to classical music turned down to 1
Dymphna

Find yourself having to go to plan B a lot?
Elspeth

Ever do that thing where you say some bit of small talk and the other person doesn't hear you over and over and you finally have to scream it out at the top of your lungs, and they get all annoyed because it wasn't all that important in the first place?
Gabrielle

Got one of those loose-knit
snoods for your Rasta hairdo?
Janet

Always inviting people to do stuff with you?
Joanna

Like your coffee so strong you
can start your car with it?
Kathleen

Did you really just drink a gallon of mountain dew?
Serena

Are you a judge or a priest?
Robyn

Do you long for more sophisticated Bostonian jokes?
Bianca

Are you a coal miner?

Gwyneth

Is your goal in life to die happy?
Meredith

When you go to the confessional does the priest
roll his eyes and give you one "our father"?

Tamsin

Ever ran a stud service for sheep?
Ramona

Damn near failed that Hebrew studies class?

Judy

Is your personality somewhere
between a dick and an asshole?
Jody

Did I just sink your battleship?

Jeanine

Do you find it depressing living out in the desert?
Adrienne

Is life just pure, relaxing joy to you?

Alyssa

Have you ever served your own parents with a
lawsuit?

Susan

Ever got to experience the thrill of a
successful prostitution sting operation?

Janelle

Do the birds go nuts whenever you
belt out your favorite Irish torch song?

Danica

Do you just live for the gorgeous
head on that first beer of spring?

Mavis

Was that last epilady treatment a little
too hard on your sensitive skin?

Moira

Are you the kind of family that pulls out the giant
deep-fat turkey fire-hazard pot every November?

Freya

Looking for a pill to take the edge off that roid rage?

Madison

Stumped?
Look for the answers at
http://www.epidemicbooks.com/StupidNames

www.ingramcontent.com/pod-product-compliance
Lightning Source LLC
LaVergne TN
LVHW021352080426
835508LV00020B/2243